Robert E. Hammond

Hammond

ltimore's streets. A car of the Edmondson and Fulton avenues line with driving. The photo was made nearly 60 years ago.

ker horsecars ran on the York Road for a while during the 1870's. e cars on the fifteen independent lines throughout the city resembl low. The drivers stood on the open platform in all kinds of weath

A CENTURY IN THE SUN

PHOTOGRAPHS OF MARYLAND

Baltimore A-rabs
1928
PHOTOGRAPHER UNKNOWN

Left. *They load up:
watermelons, cantaloupes,
peaches. They go off in
different directions, on routes
traversed since who can
remember when? They are
urban nomads, passing
through the streets singing
exotic songs of vegetables.
They are stout enemies of
modern convenience; they
survive happily, defying
progress. They tend their
ponies in the twilights.*

Land of fog
1997
PERRY THORSVIK

Preceding page. *The
Blackwater National Wildlife
Refuge emerges slowly from
the mist.*

What makes a community?
1998
AMY DAVIS

    Above. *"There's a church, there's a store ..." Third-graders at Harford Heights Elementary School, asked to describe their East Baltimore neighborhood, consult their notebooks. Yes, they're all boys. Harford Heights is a co-ed school with single-sex classes.*

Pope at prayer
1995
CHIAKI KAWAJIRI

    Preceding page. Pope John Paul II kneels in the Basilica of the Assumption during his visit to Baltimore.

Posting stats
1966
PAUL M. HUTCHINS

As the Orioles drive toward
their World Series victory, two
fans post score on an antique
truck outside City Hall.

The generations
1995
MICHAEL LUTZKY

Overleaf. *Marjorie Nagle,
whose parents opened Simmons
General Store in Snydersburg in
1924, regards granddaughter
Kristen with her ice cream cone.
Seventy-five years later, it still
tastes good.*

Proud netter
1953
A. AUBREY BODINE

Above. *Warren Hudgins steers for the fishing grounds.*

Sailing into the sky
1950
A. AUBREY BODINE

Opposite. *The Doris Hamlin out on the bay.*

Stop the action
1942
ROBERT KNEISCHE

Above. Sun *photographer Joseph DiPaola Jr. leaps from a desktop to the arms of colleague Edward Nolan at the* Sunpaper's *photo lab as he and his colleagues test a new flashbulb.* Sun *photographers Leroy Merriken and John Stadler watch the high jinks.*

National Aquarium
in Baltimore
1990
GARO LACHINIAN

Preceding page. *With 10,000 animals representing 600 species of aquatic life, Baltimore's shrine to the world of water has bottlenose dolphins leaping with joy.*

Baltimore A-rabs
1928
PHOTOGRAPHER UNKNOWN

Left. *They load up: watermelons, cantaloupes, peaches. They go off in different directions, on routes traversed since who can remember when? They are urban nomads, passing through the streets singing exotic songs of vegetables. They are stout enemies of modern convenience; they survive happily, defying progress. They tend their ponies in the twilights.*

Land of fog
1997
PERRY THORSVIK

Preceding page. *The Blackwater National Wildlife Refuge emerges slowly from the mist.*

Timekeeper

1997

AMY DAVIS

Master horologist Rowland W. Fontz tunes the great clock on the Bromo Seltzer Tower. Grandson comes to help out.

Let it first be said that this book, "A Century in The Sun," is the superb work of journalists.

Journalists whose primary tool is not a pen but a camera.

Journalists who have documented our lives and times, warts and all.

Journalists who have earned the right to be called photojournalists, using the camera as their notebook.

They are our eyes to worlds around us, recording scenes that we often overlook because we do not have their uncanny ability to see what is often right in front of us. That's what sets them apart — their unerring eye.

Much of the work is fascinating and exhilarating. Take, for instance, the cover photograph by Hans Marx. It's a wonderful shot of the Chesapeake Bay Bridge, which offers us a sense of place that actually and metaphorically links the two parts of Maryland separated by water.

One of the joys of the journey through this book is discovering the works of Marx and other talented *Sun* photojournalists as they documented how we've lived, how we've worked, what we've seen and what's mattered to us during the last 100 years. Newspaper photographs often say as much by what they show as by what they don't show.

This book is the result of an exploration — an exploration of some 1.2 million photographs in *The Sun* library.

Some were found in files covered with the dust of decades; others, often prized prints, showed the wear and tear, the scratches and creases, of frequent use. Because it was impossible to examine all of so vast a hoard, we had to resort all too often to random blind pulls, knowing that for every treasure rescued from oblivion many more remain for future spelunkers.

We sought pictures that captured people as much as history, that snapped glimpses of Maryland as delineated in an instance as well as Maryland eternal.

Photojournalism draws us closer to life as it is lived than most disciplines and has the power to unleash our emotions and our memories.

Many of the photographs in "A Century in The Sun" do just that. We hope you enjoy seeing them as much as as we enjoyed selecting them. Most of all, we're proud of the outstanding photojournalists who made them.

PREFACE

By MICHAEL E. WALLER : PUBLISHER, THE SUN

CONTENTS

The Book Staff

Editor : Joseph R. L. Sterne   *Photography Editor* : Amy Deputy   *Design Editor* : Joseph Hutchinson

Archival Researcher : Dee Lyon   *Photography Researchers* : Paul McCardell, Eugene Balk

Writing Editor : Richard O'Mara

Assistant Picture Editor : Jeffrey F. Bill

Project Manager : Deborah Golumbek

Production Manager : Jennifer Halbert

Published by *The Baltimore Sun*,
501 North Calvert Street,
Baltimore, Maryland 21278.

Library of Congress
Cataloging-in-Publication Data
applied for.

ISBN 1-893116-04-2

A CENTURY IN THE SUN

PHOTOGRAPHS OF MARYLAND

LIGHT FOR ALL

THE BALTIMORE SUN

NATURE

By TOM HORTON

Though Maryland lacks mangrove swamp and desert, Big Sur ocean headlands and a single lake gouged by glaciers, the natural range of the nation's ninth-smallest state is impressive.

From Atlantic beach to boreal peat bogs of the Appalachian Plateau; from Chesapeake mud flats to Muddy Creek Falls, plummeting 54 feet in far-western Garrett County; from oyster reefs to ski slopes; from pelican colonies to the haunts of black bears; from blackwater cypress swamps to autumn-brilliant groves of sugar maples; from the rare wildflowers that bloom on dry, shale barrens of the upper Potomac to the lush, underwater grass meadows of Tangier Sound that blossom with the olives, ivories and cerulean blues of shedding softcrabs — all this is diversity in abundance.

Maryland's nature is profoundly liquid. About a quarter of the 7.9 million acres within state boundaries is water and wetlands, including 42 rivers.

The state's meandering southern border is defined by the Potomac, a river whose bygone giant sturgeon supported a caviar factory near the District of Columbia, and whose spring shad runs helped George Washington offset bad crop years at Mount Vernon.

To the north the Susquehanna carries water from more than 20 million acres in New York and Pennsylvania. The river is the source of half of Chesapeake Bay's fresh water, and carved the deep channel that ships follow from Norfolk, Va., to Baltimore.

During Tropical Storm Agnes in June 1972, the Susquehanna filled the bay in one week with more sediment than it normally receives in 40 years. Perhaps the storm with greatest impact was the August 1933 hurricane. It cut the inlet that allowed Ocean City to become a premiere resort.

The most remarkable aspect of our watery nature may be the length of shoreline where Chesapeake Bay and its tidal rivers edge and penetrate the land. There are 4,422 miles in all!

This investiture of tidewater into the landscape has created a predominant landform, the peninsula. Examples: the Delmarva Peninsula that includes the Eastern Shore; the Southern Maryland counties of St. Mary's and Calvert peninsularized by the Potomac and Patuxent rivers; the Broadneck and Annapolis peninsulas of Anne Arundel County; the Back River Neck in Baltimore County; and the endlessly indented shorelines of the Eastern Shore.

Maryland's wildlife is notable for mass migrations, some spectacular, others barely known. Wintering waterfowl connect us annually to the whole continent — tundra swans flying in from Alaska's North Slope,

Canada geese winging from Hudson Bay, and ducks from the central Canadian prairies. In the spring, from as far as Central America, ospreys and a spectacular array of ibis, herons, egrets and other wading birds arrive for the summer.

In the waters, shad and herring return each spring from as far north as the Bay of Fundy, and striped bass weighing as much as a hundred pounds return from all over the East Coast to spawn. In late fall, great masses of eels leave from virtually every stream and river of the bay region to spawn and die in the Sargasso Sea.

In Central Maryland, the landscape is anchored by 1,280-foot Sugarloaf Mountain. Its peak presents a Piedmont vista of winding little roads, green meadows and historic barns and fences.

A lovely treasure is the vast Blackwater National Wildlife Refuge in Dorchester County. It is possible to paddle shallow-draft canoes and kayaks completely across the county, east-west, a distance of some 50 miles, without a single portage.

"Maryland's Everglades," lower Dorchester has been called. Its vast prairies of marshgrasses reflect every nuance of light and breeze, capturing the mood of the days and the seasons and the weather like some exquisitely responsive artist's canvas.

Then there is Smith Island, several miles out in Chesapeake Bay, Maryland's only offshore community. Its unique charm lies in the evolution over three centuries of humans dependent on their natural surroundings — a wonderful stew of allegiance to crabs and oysters, God and independence, a lifestyle long since vanished from most of the modern world.

Finally, the nature of Maryland is constantly changing. Species released here accidentally, like nutria and mute swans and nonmigratory Canada geese, are flourishing to the point of becoming environmental threats. Natives like white-tailed deer and beaver are adapting so well to suburbia as to become nuisances.

Oysters, 99 per cent depleted from the bay, are now the targets of rebuilding efforts.

After damming rivers for 150 years, Maryland, Pennsylvania and Virginia are now breaching dams to restore migratory fish runs.

The ravages of strip mining in Western Maryland are being repaired and reforested, even as development clears ever more forestland from the Baltimore-Washington corridor.

And even the most enduring icon of natural Maryland, Chesapeake Bay, is on the move, responding to a global sea level rise of a foot a century or more, innundating marshes, eroding islands.

On the Pocomoke River 1989

DAVE HARP

The mist glides in and closes on the brave, rooted tree; it consumes the moving forest. Nothing stops its diaphanous advance.

Frederick Valley
1938
PHOTOGRAPHER UNKNOWN

From the heights of Sugarloaf Mountain, the Frederick Valley spreads forth in all its lushness.

Eastern Neck
Wildlife Refuge
1998
LARRY C. PRICE

Overleaf. *The open sky above, the horizon's relentless retreat. A world of water below, and here and there fragments of Kent County land imbedded in the silver bay.*

Fences
1953
A. AUBREY BODINE

Above. *Rail fences zigzag through the warm hay.*

Barns
1945
A. AUBREY BODINE

Opposite. *Along Liberty Road in Baltimore County.*

Oh, deer!
1997
JED KIRSCHBAUM

Not really, just a two-piece decoy to catch poachers.

Levitation
1997
DOUG KAPUSTIN

*A deer makes its getaway
near Clarksville.*

Aloft over Smith Island
1999
JED KIRSCHBAUM

A beat of wings at twilight, heard above the water washing against a dockpost. A visitor has come from the sky, briefly inspecting us.

Patapsco Flats
1954
HANS MARX

The house, the bare trees, the outbuildings emerge suspended in space like a mirage in the desert, like Brigadoon on the Patapsco.

Cascade Falls
1928
PHOTOGRAPHER UNKNOWN

Opposite. *On a long ago summer's day, in a state forest reserve ...*

Migration
1997
PERRY THORSVIK

Magruder Landing, Prince George's County. Three trumpeter swans who believe this plane is their mother begin their 103-mile migration to Dorchester County.

Meandering
1997
PERRY THORSVIK

Above. *Twisting and gliding clear across Dorchester County, a parade of kayaks winds through a creek in the Transquaking River watershed.*

Flash
1999
JERRY JACKSON

Left. *All out on a mountain bike trail at Loch Raven, an oasis of leafy trails and a premier reservoir.*

Locust Point
1951
JOSEPH DIPAOLA JR.

Above. *A hot day, cool water, an old hulk and boys falling and jumping from the prow like ants off a popsicle stick.*

Light up the city
1954
PHOTOGRAPHER UNKNOWN

Opposite. *Suddenly there was light, and noise and electricity, and Baltimore is revealed in the night.*

Life in a bucket
1997
CHIAKI KAWAJIRI

Rounding up crawfish in Bog Pipe Creek in Union Mills.

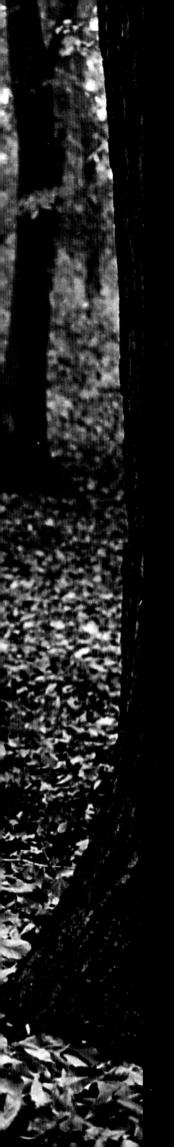

Sledding
1968
PAUL M. HUTCHINS

Above. *Up, up the hill,
then down again! In
Patterson Park.*

Autumn
1962
FRANK GARDINA

Opposite. *"If you go out
in the woods today ..."*

Ducks
1994
JED KIRSCHBAUM

Overleaf. *Wet day, nice
day for a walk, at the
Blackwater National
Wildlife Refuge.*

LIFE

By ALICE STEINBACH

Today when I look at a map of Maryland I can see that Howard County, where I spent summer weekends on my stepfather's farm, is not very far from Baltimore.

But as a child, the Saturday morning drive from the city, where we lived, to the farm in the country seemed like an endless trip to a far-away place. Growing up, I had no idea that Maryland was so small a state. The state I lived in seemed huge, an unknown country just waiting to be settled by brave pioneers willing to make the dangerous overland trek.

And why wouldn't a child think such a thing?

After all, Maryland had a great ocean to the east, mountains to the west and, in between, lakes, rivers, forests, marshes, rolling hills, fertile valleys and a bay so beautiful the sight of it prompted a child's poem. I still remember the day I sat on the bank of a creek near the bay, writing:

> *The sight of sails*
> *never fails*
> *to make me sing;*
> *Of fun, of joy,*
> *of hope, of Spring.*

I grew up here. In Maryland. In Baltimore. This is my home. This is where I rode the streetcars downtown to my tap lessons at the YWCA and caught the train to Washington at the B&O station on Mount Royal Avenue. This is where I cooled off on summer days by swimming at the beaches along the Severn River or taking drives with my family to the hills of Garrett County.

And this is where once, long before Harborplace came along, my father took me aboard a great ship moored to the docks that ran off from Pratt and Light streets like dark-stained wooden fingers.

This is where I have lived my life.

Of course, no two lives are ever the same, and no two visions of the place we inhabit as Marylanders are likely to be the same. But surely there must be some connecting threads that run through the lives we lived here in this last century; in this strangely shaped piece of land that once, before cities and towns and farms rose up, was inhabited by forests of oak, beech, black locust, hickory, pine, maple, walnut and ash.

Can you remember?

We Marylanders, quite a few of us, lived to hear the crack of a baseball bat on a summer's night and to gather around picnic tables covered with newspapers and hardshell crabs.

We lived to fish from hundreds of small bridges near hundreds of small towns and crab from piers along the small creeks that emptied into the bay.

We lived for the tailgate parties before the football games and the picnics at the point-to-point races in the Valley.

We lived for the annual summer trek to Ocean City and for the Christmas holidays when we shopped on Howard Street at Hutzler's and Hochschild's, or at the stores along Pennsylvania Avenue.

We lived for spring when restaurants put up signs announcing, "The Shad Are In."

We lived for lunch hours when we walked to the Lexington Market oyster bars or to delicatessens that served coddies on crackers.

We lived to sit with our families at outdoor concerts in the park and we lived to hear the sound of great jazz pouring out of the clubs along Pennsylvania Avenue.

And do you remember the way we would sit outside on hot, humid summer nights, the white marble steps cool against the backs of our legs?

Or how we used to walk to the corner snowball stand and watch Mr. Ford shave the ice into little paper boats, topping it with spearmint and marshmallow?

We Marylanders lived, generations of us, to catch the scent of the Atlantic Ocean, to feel the breeze off the Chesapeake Bay, to inhale the pure cold air of the mountains and to smell the pines near Deep Creek Lake.

Over the years, of course, the roads and bridges that took us to the ocean or the mountains or to our uncle's house across the bay may have changed. New towns may have sprung up where fields of corn once rippled out almost to the horizon, and suburban malls may have erased the winding back roads that once meandered past creeks and haystacks.

But our destinations have not changed. Once we get there, the ocean is still the same. And so are the mountains and rivers. And the sight of sails on the bay is as glorious as ever.

I sometimes wonder: Do we inhabit a place? Or does a place inhabit us?

A memory: *It was after supper on a summer evening and all the fathers and mothers sat outside with their children. The air was still and hot and the only sound was that of the screen door slapping shut. And then someone turned on the sprinkler and the grass grew damp and cool and your mother let you lie face down in it. And then it grew dark and the stars came out but it was still too hot to go in. So you fell asleep on the grass, wrapped in the joy of knowing this was your place in the world.*

We Marylanders lived for all that.

And we still do.

The chase
1996
KIM HAIRSTON

Tag, you're it! Mennonite School, Mount Airy.

On target
1951
HANS MARX

Opposite. *The Italian game of boccie endures, in suburb and city, anywhere you can fit a sand or clay court 75 feet long by 8 feet wide and level enough to keep the balls rolling straight.*

On stage
1958
RICHARD STACKS

Above. *Their only real instrument is the ukulele. Otherwise, wives of Baltimore Shriners use kazoos, washtubs and anything that rattles and wails, in a jazz band that entertains schools, hospitals wards — and shrine conventioneers.*

In stands
1960
ELLIS MALASHUK

Overleaf. *The pleasure of America's great game gleams from the fans' sun-filled faces. These are baseball's upper-deck angels in the glory of the afternoon at Memorial Stadium.*

Ocean City. They reach the beach at the crack of summer, full of hope and expectations. For what? Only they know. Ocean City awaits, Maryland's frenetic fun town, where only the sun sleeps and the waves leap and light dances on the metallic sea. That first morning on the sand. New swimsuits, new hair. The unveiling: "All right, girls! One! Two! Three! Last one in's a rotten egg." But watch the hair. Watch the hair! The hair! Photo by Ralph Robinson, 1964.

Crackin' crabs
1998
KARL MERTON FERRON

Above. *Five-year-old Devin Gregory goes after the backfin meat at the Maryland Seafood Festival in Annapolis.*

Beautiful swimmers
1993
JED KIRSCHBAUM

Opposite. *Pride and purpose on the Eastern Shore.*

Fences
1949
A. AUBREY BODINE

*A farmer and his horse
clip-clop down a rutted
path, by the ancient stones
of Washington County; a
boy nuzzles his happy dog.*

Wedding
1978
PHOTOGRAPHER UNKNOWN

What is a wedding? A dance, a
circle, a journey, a leap, a climb,
a beginning, a joy, a sweet sor-
row. In the end, it is a promise
of comfort. In East Baltimore.

Apron dance
1948
ALBERT D. COCHRAN

Opposite. *John Zaradroga and
his wife dance the Polish apron
dance following their wedding. A little cash in the apron for a good start.*

Baptism in the Gunpowder
1996
LINDA COAN

Overleaf. *The light is in the
water. The spirit moves in the river.
It draws the postulant into the warm
net of her people.*

Lexington Market. The clash of horns, the clop, clop of commerce, the smell of wet onions against the anarchy of market day. It's always market day in some Baltimore market: Broadway, Hollins, Belair, Cross Street. The markets were sprinkled across the city with felicitous outcome. They became knots in a great seine that drew Baltimoreans together. They continue here and there, effecting this same benign result. Some that disappeared, such as the old fish market, have been transformed into venues that offer new discoveries. Photographer unknown, 1927.

Wind
1950
ALBERT D. COCHRAN

Assault and battery by the wind reported at Lexington and Liberty streets.

Flying!
1970
ELLIS MALASHUK

Fast forward.

Scooting!
1970
PAUL M. HUTCHINS

Sedate progress.

At home
1958
RICHARD STACKS

Above. *On the porch you are half in and half out; you are open to the sun and protected from the rain. It is the ceremonial entrance to the house, the welcoming platform; it is the stage where Valerie Strott debuts before the world, just as God made her, where brother Tim struggles with the mysteries of arithmetic; it is the frontier to the republic of the family, the place where all gather to watch the end of the day.*

The street
1983
GENE SWEENEY JR.

Opposite. *At Belnord Avenue and Fleet Street, they sit before rowhouse steps scrubbed as white as healthy teeth. They sit alone and in groups. They are the sentinels of the streets.*

Family
1998
ANDRE F. CHUNG

She is the thunder, the wisdom, the rock that never wears away, is never moved. She protects, provides; she comforts, defends. She is grandmother. She is Lillie McCoy of Baltimore, guardian of six of her twenty-five grandchildren.

Screened
1994
JED KIRSCHBAUM

Opposite. *Within this painted screen, a distinctive Baltimore art form, are swans, red-topped cottages, mountain brooks and vanishing points that lead into the heart of Highlandtown.*

Crossing Guard
1948
HANS MARX

Overleaf. *That first sweet taste of civil power. That first fearful weight of responsibility as Safety Patrol Capt. Steven Ehuden controls the little kids at Baltimore's School 64 on Garrison Boulevard.*

Hot tots
1990
AMY DAVIS

It's hot. The street's hot. The house is hot.
Even the step's hot. It's hot all over
Baltimore. It's really hot in Pigtown.

Good humor in Edgewood
1995
JED KIRSCHBAUM

Left. *If it's good to eat, it's good to wear. "He's a little boy," said his mom. "When it's hot out, this is the way he is."*

Sun and smiles
1995
JED KIRSCHBAUM

Left. *Even when it's hot, you can't be too close to your good friends. Children from the Garden of Prayer Baptist Church cool off at the Druid Hill Park Pool.*

Relief
1992
MICHAEL LUTZKY

Can you see me? Do you know who I am? Four boys cool off in the fountains near the Inner Harbor.

WORK

By GILBERT SANDLER

If people can be identified by the work they do, Marylanders have changed a great deal in the years from 1900 through 2000. The work they did for the first 50 years of the century stands in sharp contrast to the work they did in the second. World War II divided the old workplace from the new.

The arrival of the 1900s saw Western Maryland and the Eastern Shore rich in farmland; the harvests would come into Baltimore from the west by truck and from the shore via the picturesque steamboats that plied the rivers and the bay.

Those waters were nurturing one of the busiest seafood industries in America, and thousands of Marylanders were employed in the state's fishing, crabbing and oystering trades.

But the work that would grow to great size and employ so many was quite different. Industrial, blue-collar work made Baltimore in its own eyes and in the eyes of the world a factory town. It would be an image hard to change; years after it has lost its accuracy, Baltimore is still regarded as a working-class kind of place. Grit is buried deep in the city's soul.

The icon of Maryland today and tomorrow may well be the computer; but yesterday it was the lunch pail.

From the late 1880s up through World War II and a few years beyond, thousands worked in Bethlehem Steel plants and in Maryland Shipbuilding and Drydock; at General Motors, Glenn L. Martin, Black & Decker, Baltimore Glass, Western Electric, and along miles of docks and loading facilities that made up the great port of Baltimore.

They worked in Baltimore's homegrown breweries — Arrow, Gunther, American, National; in the meat packing plants — Corkran Hill and Goetze's; in the shoe manufacturing and canning industries; and in the sprawling Mount Vernon-Woodberry Cotton Duck Co., at one time among the largest producers of cotton duck in the world. In many instances, sons and grandsons worked alongside fathers and grandfathers.

But not all blue-collar jobs were smokestack or mill jobs; many were in Baltimore's booming light manufacturing and, in particular, clothing production.

Before World War II Baltimore was said to be the largest center for the manufacturing of clothing, including men's hats, south of New York. Most men in America in those years wore shirts, suits, hats, coats, shoes and underwear made in Baltimore. The factories stood right in the heart of prewar downtown, side by side with movie theaters, restaurants, and retailers.

Clothing manufacturers Sonneborn and Co., L. Greif and Bro., and Schoeneman were among the largest employers in the Baltimore region, rivaling the manufacturers of steel and automobiles and power tools, and dominating the national markets.

And so when World War II came, Baltimore was perfectly positioned to become, seemingly overnight, one of the country's major mass producers of ships and planes and uniforms. With war's end came the first faint stirrings of the winds of change.

The heavy and light manufacturing that once supported the economy and that gave the city its flavor, tone and mood began to show signs of vulnerability. Worldwide changes in the economic structure hit Baltimore, and the old Baltimore standby names in manufacturing, wholesaling and retailing disappeared. As the city moved through the 1950s and 1960s, searching for an identity, its work force wandered in limbo. Jobs with decent wages contracted sharply.

By the 1970s, heavy industry began giving way to service industries, to biotech and high-tech and to the professions that serve them — law, accounting, research and development, information technology.

Maryland's colleges and universities developed programs for the highly skilled. As Baltimore changed, its workplace changed: Offices and laboratories replaced assembly line and clothing lofts. Not surprisingly, the largest employer in the state became Johns Hopkins University and Medical Institutions. Baltimore workers in a sense exchanged blue work shirts for white lab coats.

Still, Marylanders who have always kept the city functioning — teachers, police officers, firefighters, elevator operators, sanitation workers, plumbers, cabdrivers, doormen, horse trainers, oyster shuckers, librarians, bus drivers, railroad engineers, salespeople, physicians, the clergy — they are, happily, still a meaningful part of the Maryland work force. They bring Maryland stability, but not definition; they represent work that hasn't changed.

In the early part of the century, one could assess the Baltimore workplace and try to predict that the way things were was pretty much the way they would remain. In 1920 or so, that was considered (erroneously) a fairly safe bet. It isn't anymore.

Technology, communication and marketing are changing with dazzling speed. All we can safely predict is that in 100 years, in a later photographic collection of Marylanders at work, there will be a radically different set of pictures.

Fortunate farrier
1993
MICHAEL LUTZKY

If horseshoes bring luck, then Jim McIntyre had luck. From childhood on, he raced horses at the Eastern Shore's Delmar Downs, trained them in the morning, shoed them in the evening.

Welcome, hon
1995
AMY DAVIS

Preceding page. *A full-faced greeting from the ladies of the Woman's Industrial Exchange, in business since 1860 on North Charles Street.*

Water music
1938
A. AUBREY BODINE

Workers from the dockside Tilghman Island herring roe plant strum their workday to its end.

Load the looms
1938
PHOTOGRAPHER UNKNOWN

Above. *Woolen thread for the warp and woof of Baltimore's once-booming textile trade.*

City of hats
1936
PHOTOGRAPHER UNKNOWN

Opposite. *There was a time when all the boaters in Baltimore were not out on the bay but atop men's heads.*

The port of Baltimore. This is one of America's golden doors, and a highway out to the great world. From Revolutionary days the port has been an immense factor in the economy and social life of Maryland, a venue for maritime traffic and prodigious producer of ships: ships for peaceful commerce and, now and then, ships to make war. Privateers sallied from Fells Point to plunder British merchantmen in 1812. Liberty ships — 357 of them churned out in an heroic exercise of shipbuilding during World War II — carried armaments and ordnance to the Allies fighting in Hitler-dominated Europe. Cannon shot has even flown across the waters of the harbor itself, when the British came and were beaten back at Fort McHenry. These days the guns are silent, but a new kind of warfare is carried on, as Baltimore struggles against ports up and down the East Coast — Norfolk, Philadelphia, New York — for a fair slice of the economic pie. Photo by Hans Marx, 1955.

Longshoreman with his hook
1955
HANS MARX

Above. *The view from the ship's hold.*

Between decks
1955
HANS MARX

Right. *Waiting for the next sling-load of cargo.*

A cargo of fruit arrives
1936
PHOTOGRAPHER UNKNOWN

Opposite. *The San Benito unloads bananas at Pratt Street.*

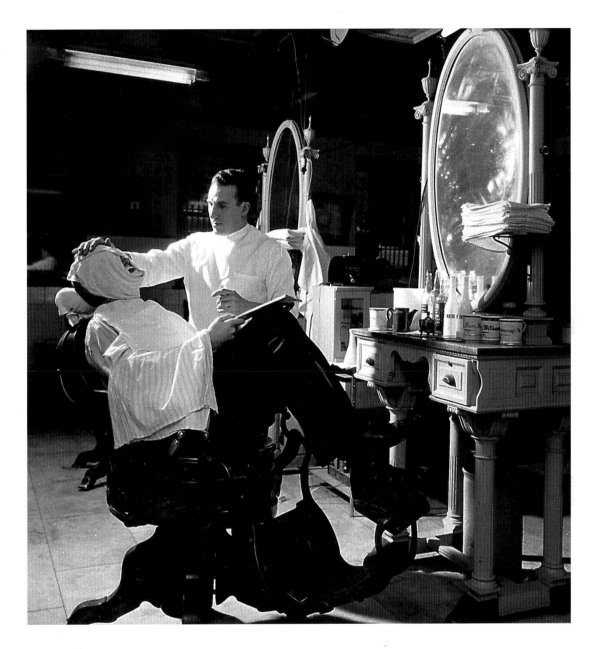

Pooch on patrol
1955
RICHARD STACKS

Opposite. *Catonsville gets combination cop and canine protection.*

Barbered in style
in Baltimore
1957
A. AUBREY BODINE

Above. *Among the amenities of the Maryland Club, long the bastion of Maryland blue-bloods, was its barber shop. Another was its famous terrapin soup, favored by Franklin D. Roosevelt and Winston Churchill.*

Schoolhouse
1952

A. AUBREY BODINE

A single room within.
The whole world without.
Last one-room school in
Frederick County. William
McGill teaches seven grades.

Hi de ho
1983
ROBERT K. HAMILTON

Baltimore-bred Cab Calloway's career took him from the Druid Hill Park neighborhood to the glittering heights of the Big Band era. He starred on Broadway and in the movies, was the source of Sportin' Life in "Porgy and Bess" and enlivened the pop music scene with his inimitable scat singing. His biggest hit, "Minnie the Moocher," was introduced in 1931.

Maestro
1998
PERRY THORSVIK

Opposite. *In his 13-year stint as director of the Baltimore Symphony Orchestra, David Zinman secured world recognition for the BSO. Here he coaches 18-year-old prodigy Hilary Hahn.*

Bessemer Furnace. Nothing ever burned so hot, or smoked so thickly or glowed so brightly, like a small sun, through the Baltimore night as Bethlehem Steel's furnaces and open hearths. The great steel-producing complex anchored at Sparrows Point was once the largest on earth. Some 30,000 workers swarmed through it like busy bees in a bright hive, day and night. It grew from its beginnings in 1890 on Patapsco's bank through decades of peace and war until it reached its apex in 1957. It was not only an industrial plant, it was a vibrant city unto itself. It deployed its own police force. It had its own school system. Housing throughout was stratified by rank in the enterprise. The work inside was hard, the nature of it at times infernal, as this 1951 photograph by A. Aubrey Bodine shows — men tilting and tugging to bring forth a bright cataract of molten steel.

Wartime boom
1942

A. AUBREY BODINE

As World War II put an end to the Great Depression, giving Americans steady jobs and paychecks that were the stuff of yearning in the 1930s, workers at the Bethlehem-Fairfield shipyard gathered one day to cheer their newfound prosperity. Then they went back to long hard days and nights, turning out Victory cargo ships that kept the lifelines open to Europe and Asia despite heavy losses to enemy submarines.

Back from the sea
1996
CHIAKI KAWAJIRI

A little paint on the anchor chain at the Bethlehem Steel shipyard.

Train man
1954
A. AUBREY BODINE

All aboard at Frederick,
as railroads stick to terra
firma in linking the state
and the nation.

Spacemen
1963
PHOTOGRAPHER UNKNOWN

*Two astronauts in the
"bug," training for a lunar
landing. Eventually the bug
evolved into the Lunar
Landing Module, from which
Neil Armstrong made his
"giant step for mankind."*

Baltimore Black Sox
1970
ELLIS MALASHUK

Laymon Yokely was one of the greatest pitchers ever — a pitcher compared with Satchel Paige, Bob Feller and Lefty Grove. After playing for Baltimore and a number of other Negro League teams, he retired and opened a shoeshine parlor on Pennsylvania Avenue.

On guard
1964
RALPH ROBINSON

Above. *Susie, on the watch at the Baltimore and Ohio yard, scares intruders away with one bark.*

Steam
1949
A. AUBREY BODINE

Opposite. *Locomotive of the Baltimore and Ohio, America's first railroad, chugs through the company's Baltimore yards.*

Watermen. The most salient feature, the topographical icon that springs to mind when contemplating the idea of Maryland is the Chesapeake Bay, created by the water trapped from melting glaciers as they withdrew following the Ice Age over 11,000 years ago. Fifty tributaries have carved its thousands of miles of shoreland. The bay and its environs, for centuries, have offered home and livelihood to watermen, who have taken rich harvests of crabs, oysters, clams, mollusks of all descriptions, rockfish, and other aquatic life. The watermen's tradition is old. It dates from the time of John Smith and the arrival of Europeans to this part of the world. Over the centuries they and their way of life have evolved into legend, embedded in the memories of the people in the bay region. But there are fewer watermen now, and their bounty from the bay is smaller. This 1990 photo by Dave Harp shows a waterman tending the jib.

Bay harvest
1999
ED KIRSCHBAUM

Above. *A Smith Island waterman ends his day with a net full of soft crabs.*

Still waters
1991
ED KIRSCHBAUM

Right. *First day of oyster season.*

Skipjack
1991

JED KIRSCHBAUM

The quintessential boat of the bay.

Gardener
1997
NANINE HARTZENBUSCH

A cup of potting soil, a dahlia,
a landscape gardening business in
good hands.

Therapist
1997
NANINE HARTZENBUSCH

For the physical therapist,
fingers search, press, stretch and
heal at Kennedy Krieger Institute.

Stylist
1997
NANINE HARTZENBUSCH

Hair-braiding Senegalese-style features flying fingers at Aissa Salon in Baltimore.

Activist
1997
NANINE HARTZENBUSCH

Love Hands Across Baltimore, now an annual event, unites people of all races and callings.

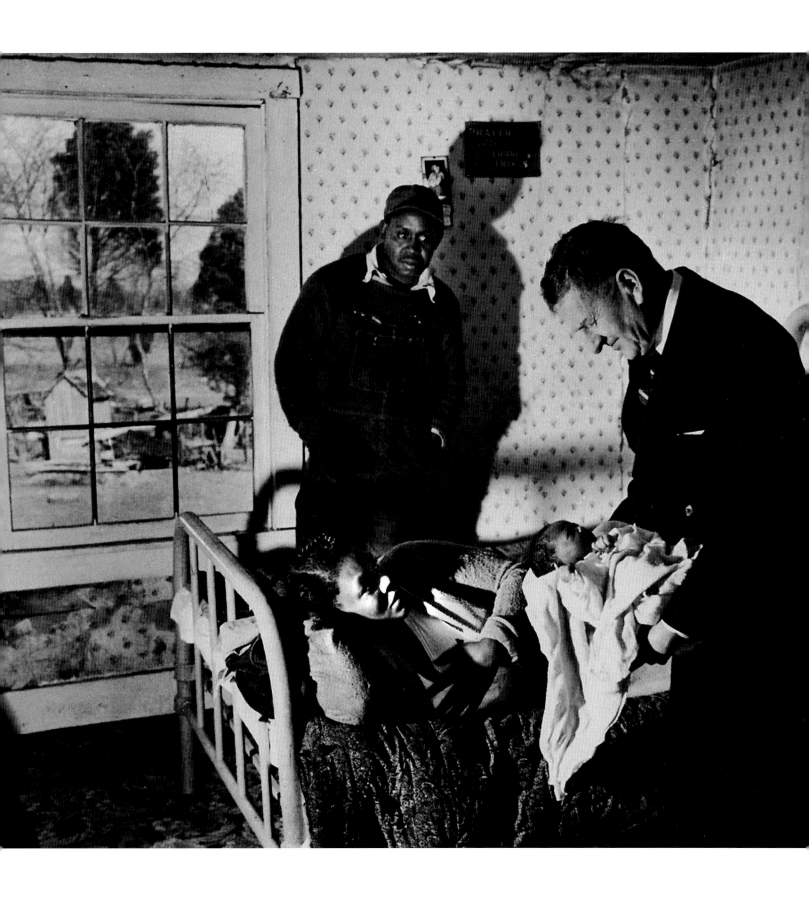

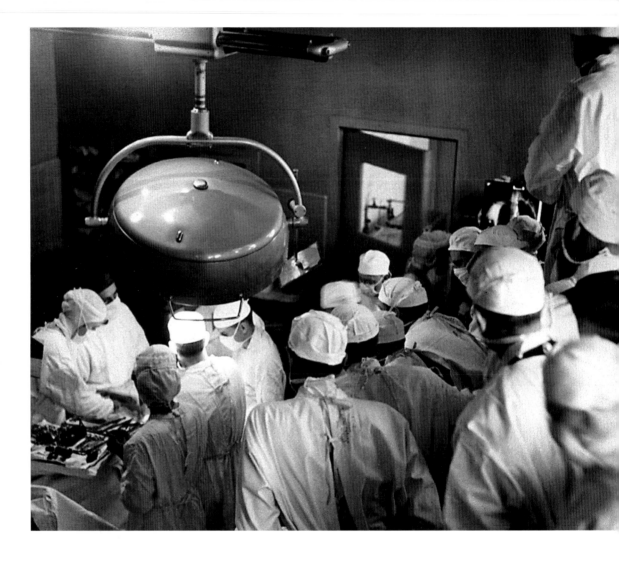

There at the beginning
1953
HANS MARX

Opposite. *Far from the hospital, a country doctor attends the birth of an Eastern Shore infant.*

A master at work
1958
EDWARD NOLAN

Above. *Johns Hopkins' famed Dr. Alfred Blalock operates while students watch.*

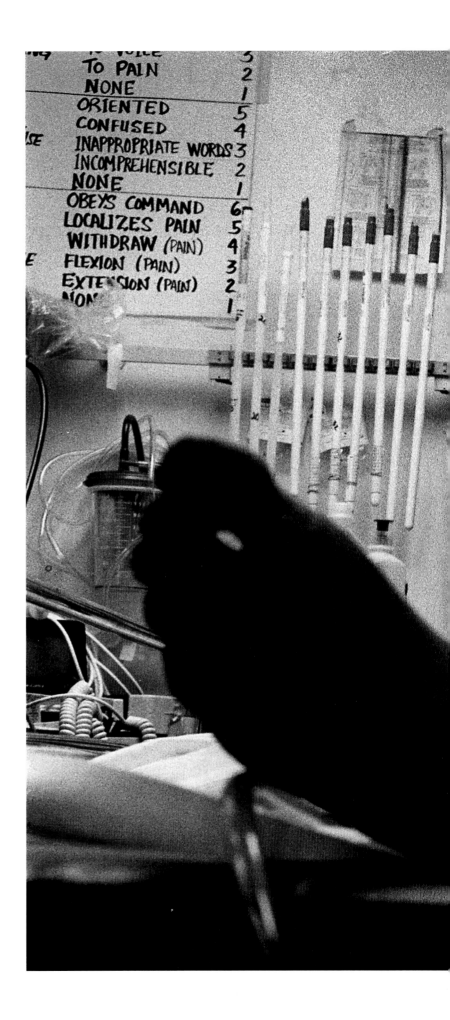

Golden hour
1988

DAVE HARP

This is the "golden hour," as Shock Trauma's pioneering founder, Dr. R. Adams Cowley, called it, the first 60 minutes after the injured arrive by helicopter to the University of Maryland Medical Center — the window of time during which lives are lost or saved. Here, Dr. Nadine Semer treats a patient stabbed three times. Innovations of the kind Shock Trauma represents have come to characterize Baltimore, which has grown into one of the country's leading health and medical treatment centers.

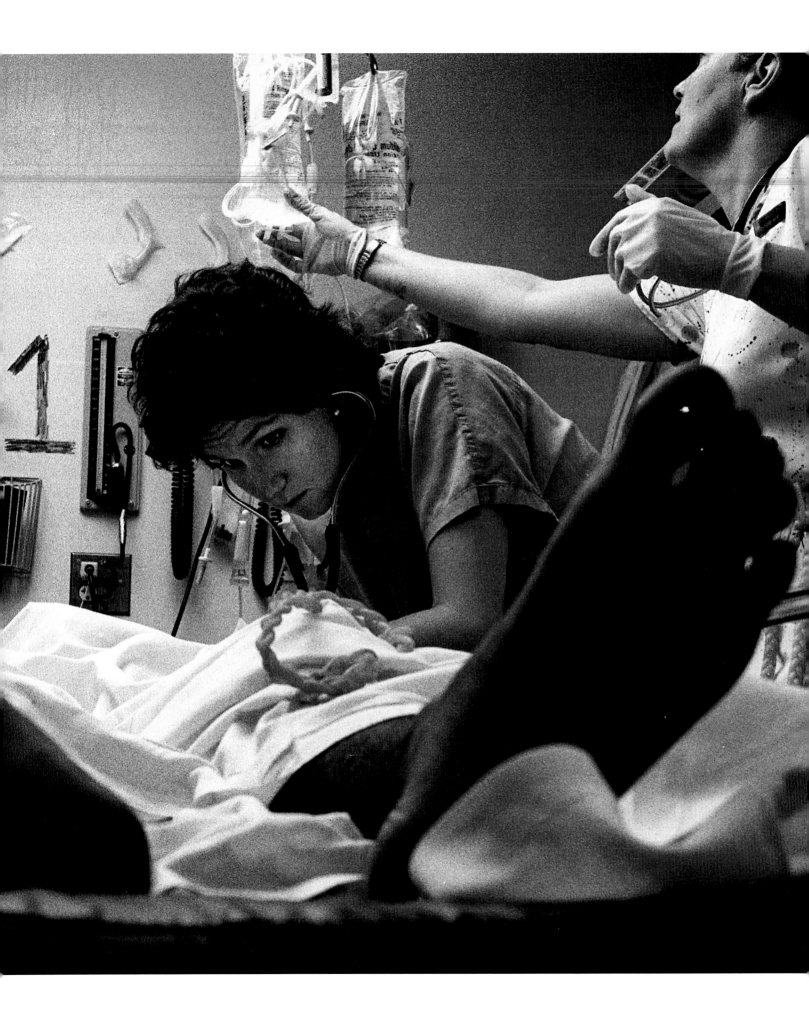

Farming. Once it was a wild Eden, this place now called Maryland. The land was shadowed by dense forests of gigantic oak and chestnut and pine. Indians pursued white-tailed deer and elk, and here and there grew a little corn or squash. Europeans came and began to farm more intensively. They cleared the land, planted the gentle rolling hills of Baltimore, Harford and Carroll counties, and even the terraces of the mountain counties, Allegany and Garrett. The Eastern Shore flourished on tobacco and soybean, then moved into chicken production. Other changes occurred: Houses grew where crops once did, and more farmland disappeared under subdivisions, served by superhighways and malls. By the century's end, suburbanization had virtually annihilated the family farm. An alarm went off, and the state government turned against destructive sprawl. Photo by A. Aubrey Bodine, 1952.

Chickens
1998

LARRY C. PRICE

A Shelltown poultry worker culls the flock, as concern rises over the birds' threat to the state's environment.

Death of a dairy farm
1997
CHIAKI KAWAJIRI

Comfort for Terry Hall from his wife, Melba, after losing their Westminster farm.

HISTORY

By PETER J. KUMPA

Everything changed. Maryland began the 20th Century as a proud society — smug, segregated, Southern-oriented. Old customs, old money, old families prevailed. Everyone in a county hierarchy had a proper place.

Only that congested smokestack of a city, Baltimore, the dynamic manufacturing, trading, educational and cultural center, disrupted the idealized pastoral way of Maryland life. It was a festering boil of a place to country people, alarming and mysterious.

As the century rolled on, much of this old Maryland was discarded or forgotten. The new Maryland was a transformed creature. It was among the top ten of the wealthiest and most-educated states, indexes of a modern and progressive society.

Those elected governor over the decades had to deal with constant transformation. Maryland had 16 of them for the 100 years, 12 Democrats and 4 Republicans.

Child labor was outlawed under the first governor of the century, John Walter Smith, a timber mogul from the Eastern Shore. The 1914 study of the state's educational system came under the first Republican governor of the century, Phillips Lee Goldsborough. Out of it, for the first time, came compulsory school attendance, certified teachers and school boards. William Donald Schaefer, first as mayor of Baltimore, then as governor, dominated the last quarter of the century.

The strong executive budget that made Maryland governors the envy of their peers across the land was designed by Frank Goodnow, president of Johns Hopkins University. It was put into place by Gov. Emerson Harrington in 1916. In the 19th century, the legislature, and particularly the original Senate, had been the masters of program and policy. No more.

Gov. Albert C. Ritchie, the first chief executive to be elected to four consecutive terms, was a stand-out. He championed state's rights, sneered at Prohibition and might have been a serious threat to Franklin D. Roosevelt's presidential nomination in 1932 but for bank failures and breadlines.

One Maryland governor did make it to the national level — alas, in lamentable fashion. Twice, in 1968 and 1972, Spiro T. Agnew was elected vice president on the ticket with Richard M. Nixon. Shortly before the Nixon resignation that would have made him president, Agnew had to leave office after pleading no contest to a single count of tax evasion.

If any individual, any governor, could be singled out for changing the course of the state, it would be William Preston Lane Jr. Elected governor in 1946, Lane moved to solve the state's severe financial problems and pent-up structural needs by pushing through a 2 percent sales tax that was to cost him re-election amid taunts of "Pennies for Lane." He got credit for taking what was a deeply conservative Southern state and transforming it into a liberal Northern model.

The list of Maryland movers and shakers goes far beyond a handful of governors. Sen. Charles McC. Mathias excelled in his goal to save the Chesapeake. As Baltimore mayor, Thomas D'Alesandro Jr. used ingenious ideas to fix the city's housing stock while pushing Charles Center and rejuvenation of the old port. Schaefer brought to completion a glittering Harborplace that attracted tourists by the busload, though the city continued to lose population.

To end historic segregation, an array of NAACP leaders fought hard battles for racial justice and equality. These included Lillie May Jackson, Clarence Jr. and Parren Mitchell and Thurgood Marshall, the first black member of the Supreme Court.

Women had to battle for voting rights — and other rights. In time, led by Mary Risteau, Maryland's women legislators would form one of the largest contingents in the nation.

So many Marylanders brought sunshine to the state in this century past. There was H. L. Mencken, who thundered in print; James W. Rouse, who built the model city of Columbia in the Howard County countryside; Louis L. Goldstein, who charmed voters and collected their taxes; Simon E. Sobeloff, who showed how government should be run. Jack Pollack left the scene as the last of Baltimore political bosses, all leveled by the television monster.

While Maryland seemed to manufacture transient characters as easily as the movies, a number of heroic institutions had lasting power. Foremost among these was Johns Hopkins University and Hospital. At the start of century, it was a pioneer in health and medicine and remained at the pinnacle of medical education at the end of it. By mid-century, a series of other institutions, such as the National Institutes of Health, the Goddard Space Flight Center and the Hubble Space Telescope, also served the world of science and humanity.

Where are we now? The Maryland historian, George H. Callcott, said it was hard to take in the grandeur of this time and place. In all of human history, he said, no people had a better chance for a better life. Concede the injustices, the ugliness, the environmental degradation, Maryland remained as ideal and beautiful a place to live as any on the globe.

Baby boom
1948
JOSHUA S. COSDEN

Above. *The first arrivals of what would prove to be the biggest generation in America's history visit the Baltimore Red Cross with their moms.*

A woman indignant
1973
RALPH ROBINSON

Opposite. *Teri O'Mera feels this is no way to advertise for a girl Friday, and pickets the Towson employment agency that devised the offensive ad.*

Salisbury riot
1933
ROBERT KNIESCHE

Not for the first time or the last, the Eastern Shore endures turmoil sparked by a lynching and racial tension. Here, National Guardsmen use tear gas to quell a jeering crowd of whites attempting to prevent the transport of the accused to Baltimore for trial.

Storm of the Century
1933
PHOTOGRAPHER UNKNOWN

*It came in like a lion
and went out the same
way. The great hurricane
of 1933 had no name, only
a bad attitude. It huffed
and it puffed, and it blew a
hole right through
Maryland's coastline, separating Ocean City from
Assateague, for good, for
ill, and forever.*

The Great Fire. One hundred and seventy-five years after it was founded on the banks of the Patapsco River, and named after an English lord, the city of Baltimore went up in flames. Virtually the entire downtown was reduced to a wasteland of rubble, a devastation and emptiness that anticipated later scenes of Europe's bombed cities after World War II. No one died as a direct result of the fire of 1904, which cleared the way for Baltimore's first spectacular rebirth. It re-emerged like a phoenix. At left, National Guardsmen patrol the cobbled streets of Baltimore in the aftermath of the Great Fire. Photographer unknown, 1904.

Dirigible
1936
PHOTOGRAPHER UNKNOWN

The German airship Hindenburg
floats proudly over Key Highway.
Nine months later it came down
in flames at Lakehurst, N.J.

Gate crasher
1976
LLOYD PEARSON

Opposite. *Remains of a light
plane that came to a sudden stop in
the upper deck of Memorial Stadium
in Baltimore after a Colts-Steelers
game. The pilot survived, and the
Steelers won, 40-14.*

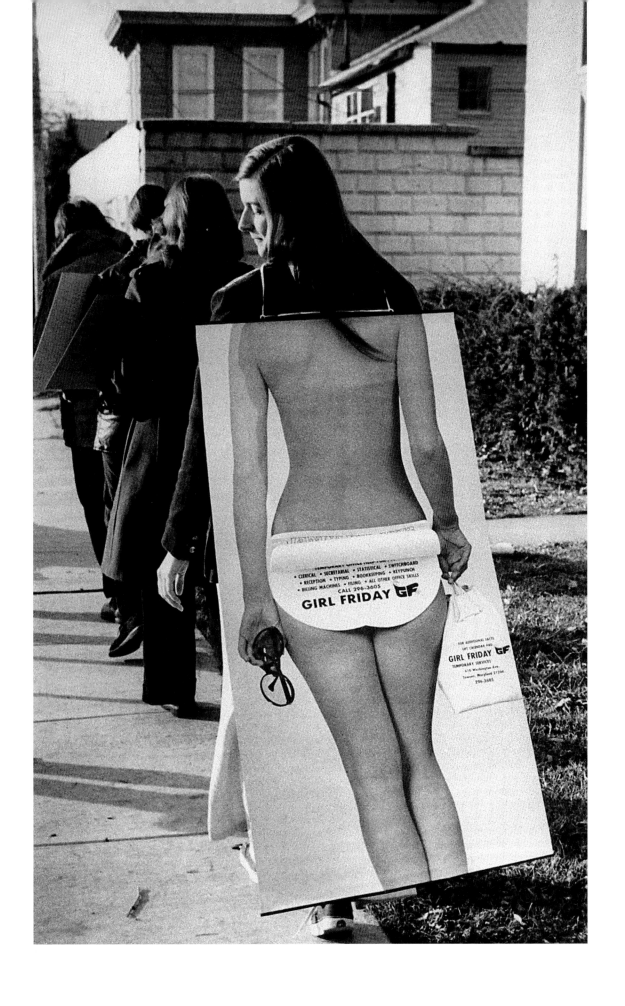

Veterans. Soldiers fell from the sky, turned corners in the grip of fear in far-off blasted cities, manned howitzers in France and lugged automatic rifles into Germany against stubborn resistance. They endured the stink of rotting bodies on hot Pacific islands, and the lethal chaos of Korea and the dispiriting uncertainty of Vietnam. The Persian Gulf war came and went, Kosovo emerged. These are the veterans, the American warriors who answered a call — and returned. They are ageless and matchless. Through the generations the uniforms change, and the faces remain the same. Resolute. Sad. Like the faces of these World War I veterans, William S. Langston, opposite, and George Manns, above, as they remembered Armistice Day, 1918, a long 75 years later. Photos by Michael Lutzky, 1993.

Training
1942
LEE MCCARDELL

*Troops from Maryland's 29th Division board transport
before their passage from the fog of England into the fog of war.*

Holocaust
1945
LEE MCCARDELL

When the U.S. Army occupied Nuremberg, Germany, they found the bodies of 161 massacred Polish Jews. The Americans ordered townspeople to view the remains and furnish pallbearers at funeral services

Surrender
1944
LEE MCCARDELL

Above. *A defeated German soldier turns himself in to American troops with the 3rd Army, at Cherbourg, France.*

Treasure
1944
LEE MCCARDELL

Left. *Three French boys display loot found in the wreckage of war: a barometer, with small figures entering or leaving the toy house depending on the weather.*

Martin Clipper
1935
PHOTOGRAPHER UNKNOWN

Above. *Having made the historic flight from San Francisco to Manila in 1935, the Baltimore-built Clipper went down in 1946.*

Forward march
1929
PHOTOGRAPHER UNKNOWN

Opposite. *Marines proudly parade on Baltimore Street as the city celebrates its bicentennial.*

Vietnam. Peace is pulverized by war for over 20 long years in Vietnam, and for much of that time the United States is involved. Protests and demonstrations of every sort, for and against the war, failed to slow the conflict, as more bombs, more planes to deliver them, more troops, more and heavier weapons fail to win it. In the end peace wins through determination, weariness, frustration and the countless multiplication of quiet appeals and strident demands that we withdraw. The decision made and implemented, Americans enter the agony of the aftermath. A GI slogs through Tay Ninh province in Vietnam as the United States sinks deeper into the conflict. Photo by Robert A. Erlandson, 1967.

Anti-war flames
1968

WILLIAM L. LA FORCE

*The Rev. Philip Berrigan,
rear left, begins his long career
as an activist for peace at a draft
card burning.*

Give war a chance
1965
WILLIAM L. LA FORCE

*As war fever rages, Johns
Hopkins students demand
greater American involvement
in Vietnam.*

Vigil
1967
LLOYD PEARSON

A candlelight ceremony against the Vietnam War before the Washington Monument in Baltimore.

Melancholy remembrance 1985

J. PAT CARTER

Thoughts of war, and death at the Vietnam monument on Federal Hill.

Looking ahead. Turmoil came to the quiet town of Cambridge on Maryland's Eastern Shore in 1964. The spirit igniting civil rights protests all across the country had spread electrically into that region of the state where the hold of Jim Crow was strongest. People marched, presenting themselves for arrest for violating racist laws. Violence erupted; hatred filled the air like an explosive gas. In Cambridge the National Guard came and imposed its rigid peace. And in that quiet, slackwater time between outbursts, a child wanders by. Photo by George Cook, 1964.

Freedom song
1963
RICHARD CHILDRESS

Above. *After a day of demonstrating at Gwynn Oak Park and a night in jail, the Rev. William Dwyer, Edward Chance and the Rev. Frank Williams emerge singing: "I woke up this morning with my mind on freedom."*

Gwynn Oak Park
1963
WALTER M. MCCARDELL

Opposite. *And still another defeat for Jim Crow. Baltimore civil rights leaders invite arrest while demonstrating for the desegregation of the amusement park.*

The King
1964
PHOTOGRAPHER UNKNOWN

*The Rev. Dr. Martin Luther King Jr.
arrives in Baltimore to urge African-
Americans to vote in the impending presidential election.*

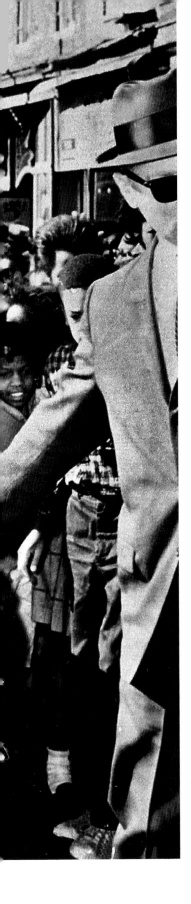

Mule train
1968

PAUL M. HUTCHINS

In those days of ferment and civil rights rallies, the Rev. Ralph David Abernathy (waving) rides a "freedom wagon" along Moser Street in Baltimore.

George Wallace
1968
LLOYD PEARSON

Above. *The segregationist Alabama governor, later shot and crippled at a Maryland shopping center, makes a point while running for president ...*

Hagerstown rally
1972
RALPH ROBINSON

... and, right, *draws a response from a different crowd four years later.*

On his own
1968

LLOYD PEARSON

Much of Baltimore lay broken and bruised following the riots that erupted in response to the assassination of the Rev. Martin Luther King Jr., and that put the National Guard on the city's streets. Order at last restored, a Baltimore police officer stands guard at Gay and Orleans.

Tradition of protest
1998
ELIZABETH MALBY

Kweisi Mfume, a former Baltimore Congressman and the president of the NAACP, follows in the path of so many others, as he presents himself for arrest before the Supreme Court, in protest against its discriminatory hiring practices.

Politicians. Who are these people? Are they different from the rest of us? Are they shallow, self-absorbed careerists forever feathering their nests, justifying the whining of cynics? ("Politicians are all the same! Ya can't trust 'em.") Or are they dedicated servants of us all, people who sacrifice more time than they have for their towns, cities and country, giving up family life, occasionally even personal dignity, to that end? William Donald Schaefer was exuberant, frequently annoyed, occasionally clownish. Kurt L. Schmoke was reserved. Two entirely different styles. Theodore R. McKeldin, shown at right in a 1967 photo by William L. Klender as he signed a piece of legislation, was one of the more beloved Maryland politicians. He served as the mayor of Baltimore, then governor of Maryland, then returned again as mayor. He had a high-toned oratorical style, understood the nuances of governing (he revised the City Charter), and had a common touch he never lost. He and Schaefer and Schmoke answer the first question asked above. Politicians are like us. They are us.

Boom!
1940
PHOTOGRAPHER UNKNOWN

The guns of Aberdeen Proving Ground are too much for President Franklin Roosevelt, Maj. Gen. Charles M. Wesson and Gov. Herbert O'Connor, during a inspection of the Army's weapons testing facility.

Political monkeyshines
1987
BARBARA HADDOCK-TAYLOR

House Speaker Clayton Mitchell, Gov. William Donald Schaefer and Senate President Mike Miller hear no evil, see no evil, speak no evil during a light moment in legislative battles.

Maryland's favorite son
1932
PHOTOGRAPHER UNKNOWN

Above. *Supporters from the 5th District, 27th Ward, demonstrate support for Gov. Albert C. Ritchie's presidential candidacy outside Mount Royal Station as he heads for the Democratic nominating convention in Chicago .*

Bringing up the rear
1968
WILLIAM L. KLENDER

Opposite. *Backside salute to the Republican ticket of Richard Nixon and Maryland's Spiro Agnew.*

Camelot aborning. It is 1960. It was a new time and suddenly there was a new face, a new idea, a New Frontier promised. John F. Kennedy, a Roman Catholic backed by an Irish-American fortune, declares for the presidency, and wins. He seizes the imagination of Americans unaccustomed to his kind of glamour in their politicians. He raises the aspirations of ordinary people, in places like this, the Westview Shopping Center. He sends Peace Corps volunteers around the world, rallies to the defense of African-Americans demanding fair treatment; he faces down the Soviets; then his life is gone. He remains for many a shining memory. Photo by Joseph DiPaola Jr., 1960.

They like Ike
1952
ALBERT D. COCHRAN

Above. *Perched on a balustrade at Mount Vernon Square, twirling their umbrellas, holding tight to tethers on a giant Ike balloon, five Eisenhower enthusiasts show off for the Grand Old Party.*

The president
1998
JED KIRSCHBAUM

Left. *President Bill Clinton addresses the crowd at the Pleasant View Gardens' Boys and Girls Club in East Baltimore.*

Nixon exultant
1970
WALTER M. MCCARDELL

Right. *President Richard Nixon gives double victory sign at a rally in East Baltimore with Sen. Charles McC. Mathias and Rep. J. Glenn Beall.*

Give 'em hell
1948
ROBERT KNIESCHE

Below. *On his way to the biggest political upset of the century, President Harry Truman rallies Baltimore voters at the Pennsylvania Railroad yards.*

The mayor celebrates
1987
IRVING J. PHILLIPS JR.

Clarence Du Burns makes history as the city's
first African-American mayor. In a pivotal year,
he was City Council president and fill-in mayor
before losing to Kurt L. Schmoke.

Oysters aweigh
1963
WILLIAM H. MORTIMER

Long-serving I
Goldstein, state con
with giant oyster sh
Choptank River, fr
state's rehabilitati

Smack of kisses
1987

AMY DAVIS

Baltimore's first elected African-American mayor, Kurt L. Schmoke, pecks his wife, Patricia, at the 1987 victory celebration. Schmoke served three terms.

Dancing duo
1984
JED KIRSCHBAUM

Opposite. *Mayor William Donald "Nijinsky" Schaefer, takes the delicate hand of Rep. Barbara "Pavlova" Mikulski at the Baltimore School for the Arts.*

'Pretty good, not bad.'
1933
FRANK MILLER

Above. *H.L. Mencken, the great Disturber of the Peace, hoists one to mark the passing of Prohibition, all in all, he thought, a bad idea whose time had finally gone.*

Ritual

By Carl Schoettler

The rituals of the year, whether small and personal or large and communal, define our lives in myriad ways — as children, parents, students, players or spectators, diners and drinkers, merrymakers and mourners. They define us as a community, a people and a nation.

On the Fourth of July, Independence Day, our oldest national holiday, we celebrate the founding of the nation with fireworks, cookouts — and discount sales. On Presidents Day, we honor the great leaders of our country, especially George Washington, the founder, and Abraham Lincoln, the preserver, of our union of diverse and disparate peoples. And we hold more sales.

We mourn fallen heroes from old wars on Memorial Day — and pray that no more wars come to claim our young. And here in Maryland we flock to Ocean City in celebration of the beginning of our season in the sun.

We cheer lustily on baseball's opening day at Camden Yards and at the arrival of the football season at Ravens stadium — and for the return of lacrosse to practically every college and high school in Maryland.

These are the recurrent moments *Sun* photographers have recorded faithfully for nearly a century now — faithfully and resourcefully and brilliantly.

But the rituals that recur annually in our lives are among the toughest of assignments for a newspaper photographer.

When the groundhog pops up for his annual prediction about winter, he's apt to be be greeted by a couple of platoons of photographers. And they've been taking pictures of his toothy visage for decades. Trying to find a fresh image is harder than winning a publications promotion sweepstakes.

In a century of photography, how many pictures have been taken at Fourth of July celebrations? The challenge for the photographer who tries to capture the rhythms of our lives is to avoid the routine, the banal and the cliche.

Sun photographers have been downright heroic in conquering the temptation to surrender to routine kitsch. And for years they worked anonymously. *The Sun* began to credit photographers regularly in the daily paper only in the 1960s.

They've nonetheless managed to create small works of art on deadline. On Memorial Day, for example, they honor our war dead and celebrate Americana in photos of folksy small-town parades.

As summer ends, we pass a family milestone when we take our children to school for their first day. And it takes a dedicated photographer to search for the heart of the community in its young people.

We go to the Maryland State Fair in late summer and rejoice in the old-time agrarian quality that still survives in the barns and judging rings at Timonium. Years later we find again in a photograph the swirl of nighttime excitement of Ferris wheels whirling in the lowering sky like huge steel gems.

Our rituals wax and wane with the seasons and the years.

We marry in June and we measure the passing of our lives with the great religious holidays — the holy days of the year: Rosh Hashana and Yom Kippur, Easter and Christmas, Kwanzaa and Ramadan — and in the secular festivals of the Flower Mart, the society fest of the point-to-point at My Lady's Manor and the plebeian zest of the infield at Pimlico for the running of the Preakness.

We mark our military victories and defeats at North Point and Antietam and Frederick.

We bask in the diversity of our ethnic heritage on St. Patrick's Day and St. Andrew's Day and at the Greek festival of St. Nicholas Orthodox Church and the Polish festival in Patterson Park and at Afram around the Inner Harbor and at spaghetti dinners at St. Leo's and salsa fiestas in Fells Point and at dozens of other annual celebrations around the city and state.

The photographs often become as classic as the ceremonies of life they capture and as worthy of savoring again and again as the first crab of the year and the first hot dog on opening day and the taste of champagne as the old year wanes and the New Year arrives and we repeat again the rituals we love.

Sans Big Top
1966
RICHARD STACKS

Opposite. *The ladies of the circus wait in the wings as the Ringling Bros. Barnum and Bailey Circus rolls on into its future. Though the big canvas tents are now a part of its history, the show is still the Greatest on Earth. Now it unfolds its three rings in ball parks, civic centers and armories. But fliers fly, lions roar, acrobats tumble and clowns fall down.*

Pimlico
1994
CHIEN-CHI CHANG

Preceding page. *It is the eighth race. The field advances. Preakness!*

Hitting the hay — with heifer
1994
GEORGE W. HOLSEY

Above. *Nap time at the annual state fair in Timonium.*

Carnival life
1996
CHIAKI KAWAJIRI

Opposite. *On the road, at rest, at Timonium, a mother hugs her daughter as grandmom looks on.*

The prom
1979
JED KIRSCHBAUM

For those who remember.

A town of tribes
1989
JED KIRSCHBAUM

Above. *Baltimore is a place of ethnic pockets, neighborhoods both intact and in disarray. It exhibits the cosmopolitanism of all great cities: It is rich, it is poor; it is strong, it is weak: it is white and black and brown and red. Poles, Jews, Greeks, Germans, Russians, Mexicans, Guatemalans, Koreans, Chinese, all work and play in a grand racial profusion. The links among these peoples are sometimes fragile, sometimes strong. Baltimoreans celebrate their uniqueness at festivals and street fairs, for which the city has become mildly famous. Here, at a Jewish festival, dancers take exception to the notion of the melting pot, and always have. Baltimore was diverse before diversity was chic.*

Opening Day
1997
GENE SWEENEY JR.

Overleaf. *Future Hall-of-Famer Cal Ripken Jr. runs a gantlet of friendly hands before the home opener of the season.*

The Flower Mart. William Howard Taft was president. James H. Preston had just taken office as mayor of Baltimore. And the ladies of the Baltimore Civic League and the Home and Garden Club decided the time was at hand to celebrate the coming of spring in proper fashion. On May 4, 1911, the first Flower Mart was held. Tradition piled on tradition through the years. Lemon sticks became perennial. Crab cakes and fried oysters now compete with hot dogs, pizza and even fried dough. Everything is different; everything is the same. Photographer unknown, 1928.

Day of the Irish. In America Ireland is more a thought than a place, a shimmering if not entirely accurate idea of loamy green fastness sprinkled with secret dark places, esoteric lore and mouldering old monasteries where the wisdom of the classical world was preserved. On St. Patrick's Day the idea of Ireland takes hold of all and any who claim even the slightest attachment to the island. Expectations are great, as one can see on the faces of these dreamers at the Irish Pub in East Baltimore. This moment was captured in 1974 by William H. Mortimer.

Memorial Day. A time to remember those gone in the nation's wars, their lives lost and never lived; time to recall the faces from the past before they fade for good, to listen for the voices that so animated us and through which we lived parts of our own lives. Time to read their names carved on the wall, or walk among the white stones' evidence of war's grim consequence. Time to gather flowers. Sit quietly. Photo by Richard Stacks, 1957.

Proud parade watcher
1980

JED KIRSCHBAUM

Above. *Towson.*

Color guard
1953

WILLIAM L. KLENDER

Opposite. *Catonsville.*

Don't want to go
1995
KIM HAIRSTON

Above. *William Herd, facing his first day at school, clings to his mom like a barnacle.*

Naval Academy
1980
JED KIRSCHBAUM

Opposite. *First women graduates making waves.*

Up and away
1999
ALGERINA PERNA

Preceding page. *Morgan University students on that last, happy day.*

Slippin' and slidin'
1997
JOHN MAKELY

Named for Commander W.L. Herndon, who went down with his ship in 1857, the obelisk that honors him is the focus of events during the Naval Academy's annual Commissioning Week. It is smeared with lard and the first plebe up its slippery sides with the aim of replacing a plebe's "dixie cup" with an upperclassman's cap. The one who succeeds, it is believed by some, will become the class' first admiral.

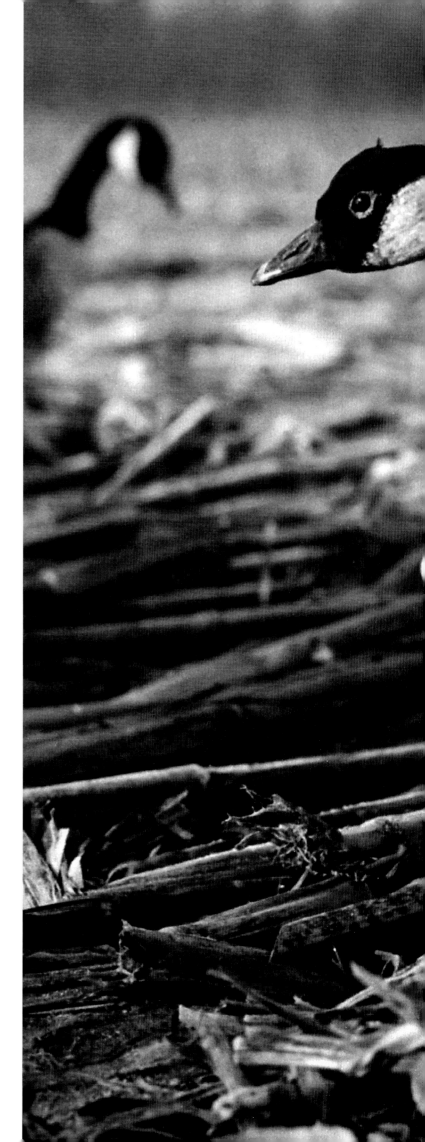

Ducks and geese better scurry
1962

RICHARD STACKS

Lying in wait, hunched down in ambush, decoys deployed, the hunters wait in their cold, damp misery. They are warmed only by their expectations, their hopes for a bird on the table. Here they come! First you hear them, then you see them in the early sun. They fly closer. Forty yards away; it's a tough shot. Thirty yards. All eyes are up!

The sand ponies
1954
HANS MARX

    The story goes that the ponies of Assateague Island came off a Spanish ship, one of many over the centuries destroyed in storms off the coast. They swam to this rough, wind-raked shore, and survived. Life was hard, but they endured, and even thrived in the good years. Eventually, they found a permanent home in the legend of this place, in tales such as "Misty of Chincoteague," the children's classic for every kid who dreams of owning his or her own pony.

SPORT

By JOHN STEADMAN

Everything about sports in Maryland during the past century creates a contrast in emotion: the loss of major league franchises in three sporting pursuits, recovery of two of them with the building of veritable stadium-palaces with $500 million in public money and the belief, in the end, that Baltimore has taken on a new glow and a better self-image.

It has been an oft-stated impression that if a city doesn't have a big-league baseball identity, it is nothing more than East Bridgeport.

An American League club returned to Baltimore in 1954, amid parades and celebrations, when the moribund St. Louis Browns, fighting bankruptcy, were sold to a group of Baltimore boosters. A dozen years later the Orioles won their first World Series.

The wait for big-league status had lasted 51 years — a downtime when Baltimore had to content itself with membership in the Eastern and International Leagues. Often mocked as a "minor league town," Marylanders at least could retort: "But what other city contributed Babe Ruth?"

Although Baltimore lost big league baseball from 1902 to 1954, the local minor league franchise under owner-manager Jack Dunn was the winningest dynasty the sport has ever known. The Orioles won seven pennants in a row from 1919 to 1926 with the likes of Lefty Grove, Max Bishop, George Earnshaw, Fritz Maisel, Joe Boley, Jack Ogden and Tommy Thomas.

During the era of segregated baseball, Baltimore was represented by the Black Sox and the Elite/Giants. One player, Roy Campanella, signed with the Brooklyn Dodgers and became a Hall of Fame catcher. Another so honored (belatedly) was pitcher/utility player Leon Day.

During the first half-century of professional sports purgatory, Baltimore did shine once a year when the nation's best racehorses ran the Preakness at Pimlico — a tradition dating to the 1870s.

College football made its appearance from time to time, chiefly with the Naval Academy playing Maryland, Notre Dame and Army (in 1924, 1944 and, now, 2000).

In 1934, Western Maryland College, then a dominant collegiate football power, had the national scoring leader in Bill Shepherd, a Pennsylvania import. A home-grown All-American was Jack Scarbath of Maryland.

Professional football didn't come to Baltimore until 1947. The Colts arrived, sporting a name ideally suited because of Maryland's long romance with the horse.

The Colts built a fanatical following. Heroes included such Hall of Fame players as John Unitas, Art Donovan, Lenny Moore, Jim Parker, Raymond Berry, John Mackey and Ted Hendricks, plus coaches Weeb Eubank and Don Shula.

But the dream was shattered in 1984. Owner Bob Irsay physically transferred the team's property to Indianapolis, making the move under the cover of darkness. Strong efforts were made to regain an AFL franchise, but it was not until 1996 that the Cleveland Browns moved to Baltimore with a name-change to Ravens.

Baltimore became a hotbed for boxing in the 1920s and '30s. There were weeks when as many as five shows were presented. Baltimore was the first to have two brothers, Joe and Vince Dundee, to become champions. Other title-winners were Joe Gans, Johnny "Kid" Williams, Alvin Anderson and Dwight Braxton.

The Baltimore basketball Bullets, now the Washington Wizards, won the professional crown in 1947-1948. Player-coach Buddy Jeanette, an inspirational leader with a 10.7 scoring average, showed the way. Owner Abe Pollin, who had earlier rescued the Bullets from financial ruin, moved his franchise to Landover from Baltimore's downtown Civic Center and, ultimately, in 1997, to the MCI Center in Washington.

At one time, Baltimore was a stop on the PGA and LPGA golf tours. The Eastern Open, played for 13 years and using the courses at Mount Pleasant and Pine Ridge, had some great names as winners, including Sam Snead, Arnold Palmer and Gene Littler.

The LPGA had a longer run, from 1962 through 1980, and put such Hall of Fame names on its scoreboard as Nancy Lopez, Mickey Wright, Carol Mann, Pat Bradley and Kathy Whitworth.

Baltimore Country Club has been the leader in playing host to national championships: the U.S. Open in 1899, the PGA in 1928, the U.S. Amateur in 1932, the Walker Cup and the U.S. Women's Open in 1988.

In 1939, Mount Pleasant was selected for the U.S. Public Links Championship. So Baltimore has had its moments in the golf spotlight. Among its most proficient touring professionals were Carol Mann, Tina Barrett, Donnie Hammond, Charley Bassler, Bill Collins and Fred Funk.

The state of Maryland has long enjoyed a reputation as the "cradle of lacrosse." Johns Hopkins has been the pre-eminent power, winning 42 — yes, 42 — national championships.

Since 1971, the NCAA has conducted a post-season tournament and Hopkins has never missed being selected. The growth of the game has spread to parts of the country that once didn't know the difference between a lacrosse stick and a crab net.

Champions of the world
1966

PAUL M. HUTCHINS

The Baltimore Orioles captured their first World Series a dozen years after the return of big-league baseball to Baltimore. They did it in pulverizing style, winning four straight games over the Los Angeles Dodgers. Here the exuberance of the moment is captured as pitcher Dave McNally, wearing No. 19, celebrates the winning put-out as Hall of Fame third-baseman, Brooks Robinson, leaps skyward and catcher Andy Etchebarren rushes to join a team-wide victory dance. WOULD YOU BELIEVE IT? FOUR STRAIGHT! read the banner headline next morning.

Baseball diplomacy
1999
NANINE HARTZENBUSCH

Above. *If baseball is big in Baltimore, it's colossal in Cuba. At the second of the Orioles-Cuba home and home series in 1999, a Havana fan cheers as he celebrates their victory over the Orioles.*

Dug-out celebration
1999
KARL MERTON FERRON

Opposite. *Gabriel Perre of the Cuban all-star team celebrates their upset victory at Camden Yards. Five weeks earlier, the Orioles defeated the Cubans in Havana in the first part of the series.*

Duckpin bowling. Long before sociologists worried about people "bowling alone," Baltimore took up duckpins as a participatory sport and a bonding ritual that brought neighbors, co-workers and friends together for fun and fellowship. Here members of "The Old Stars" meet for a Friday morning of sweat and strikes. Photography by Michael Lutzky, 1994.

The incomparable No. 19
1965

PAUL M. HUTCHINS

The Baltimore Colts are the stuff of legend. Moving to Baltimore from Dallas, they suffered the usual miseries of a new franchise. But the glory years were not long in coming. Led by No. 19, Johnny Unitas, shown here fading back in classic style for another unerring pass, the Colts won back-to-back Super Bowls in 1958 and 1959. These historic triumphs turned Baltimore into a football-crazy town that had to endure the loss of its beloved team during a snowy night in 1984. Yet fans clung to their hopes despite many disappointments until big-time football metamorphosed in the form of the Baltimore Ravens a dozen years later.

Blessing of the hounds
1948
ELLIS MALASHUK

Opposite. Stately horses, yelping dogs, brilliantly attired equestrians and a crisp Maryland morning. Why, only a fox (and his humanoid friends) would be churlish enough to lament this lovely spectacle.

Horse country
1953
JOSEPH DIPAOLA JR.

Above. Horse lovers for a day or all days crowd a Washington Valley estate for the annual Maryland Hunt Club point-to-point race.

Young gentry
1952
JOSEPH DIPAOLA JR.

Above. Polly and Bunny Richards, binoculars at the ready, await the Grand National race.

Army-Navy
1924
PHOTOGRAPHER UNKNOWN

Above. *Mascots, goat and mule, meet before the first game ever played in Maryland by the cadets of West Point and the Middies of Annapolis. The two service academy football teams met again in 1944 here, and will return for a third contest to mark the new millennium.*

Terps with terrapin
1934
PHOTOGRAPHER UNKNOWN

Below. *University of Maryland fans with their own mascot: not the fastest thing on four legs, but sure to get there.*

Green Terrors
1936
PHOTOGRAPHER UNKNOWN

No nose guards, no mouth guards, no chin guards
in those days, Western Maryland College's national-
ly ranked football team, the Green Terrors, huddle.

Sailing, sailing
1997
ALGERINA PERNA

Crew members on the deck of Chessie, Baltimore's entry in the Whitbread Around the World Race, take the spray in practice maneuvers on the Chesapeake Bay.

Immortal Cal. Emotion drenched Camden Yards, no less the Iron Man it was all about, the night that short-stop Cal Ripken broke Lou Gehrig's record for most consecutive games played in the major leagues. For decades, fans thought the Gehrig streak — at 2,130 — would never be exceeded. But year after year, defying injury in an era when the disabled list became a tool of baseball management, Aberdeen's Cal Ripken kept going and going and going. On September 7, 1995, he played Game No. 2,131, and kept reporting for duty, day after day, until he sat himself down without advance notice or fanfare late in the 1998 season. He had played 2,632 games in a row, from May 30, 1982, until September 20, 1998, a record likely to last as long as baseball. Photo by Karl Merton Ferron, 1995.

Fireworks over a field of dreams
1954
RICHARD STACKS

Opposite. *Pyrotechnics in the skies and on the turf at old Memorial Stadium, home of the Orioles from 1954 through 1991, the football Colts from 1954 through 1984 and the Ravens from 1996 through 1997.*

Last game at Memorial Stadium
1991
KENNETH K. LAM

Above. *Catcher, the toughest, most grueling position in baseball by a large margin, the position of battered hands and aching knees and fierce collisions at homeplate. Catchers Elrod Hendricks and Rick Dempsey, two of the most popular players ever to wear the Orioles uniform, show what teamsmanship is all about.*

Dismayed
1982
WILLIAM HOTZ

Right. *A teary Earl
Weaver, managing his
last game, reflected
Baltimore heartbreak
when the Orioles lost the
crucial contest in a
comeback season that
would have gained them
entry to the American
League playoffs.*

Frustration
1970
PHOTOGRAPHER UNKNOWN

Opposite. *Frank
Robinson, the Triple
Crown superstar player
of championship Orioles
teams, shows his compet-
itive spirit as he contests
a third-strike call by
umpire Frank Umont.*

The Babe
1931
LEROY MERRIKEN

Left. *Baltimore-born
George Herman Ruth,
the Bambino, the Sultan
of Swat, the pride of the
New York Yankees, the
immortal Babe himself,
thrills his old hometown
during an exhibition
appearance at the old
Oriole Park, at the time
a bush-league ball field.*

Into the stretch. At the fourth turn in the 1999 Preakness, a hero of a horse, Charismatic, turns on the heat to repeat his Kentucky Derby triumph. Alas, at the Belmont three weeks later, he broke his left front leg stumbling into a third-place finish. Instead of the Triple Crown, he was retired to stud. The Preakness is Pimlico's proudest day of the year, as it has been with only a few exceptions since the 1870s. Tens of thousands of spectators and revelers crowd the grandstand and the infield as nationwide television follows the thundering herd every step of the way. Photo by Doug Kapustin, 1999.

Disputed finish
1962
JOSEPH DIPAOLA JR.

Above. In this prize-winning photo of the 1962 Preakness, one of the roughest contests in the history of the race, Greek Money on the right beats Ridan despite jockey Manuel Yeaza's jabbing left elbow.

Thoroughbred
1954
A. AUBREY BODINE

Opposite. On a misty morning at Sagamore Farms, a huge spread of green meadow and white fence in the Green Spring Valley of Baltimore County, one of the greatest racehorses of all, Native Dancer, winner of the 1953 Preakness and Belmont Stakes, walks quietly in retirement. Victor in 21 of his 22 starts, he died in 1967.

Gentry at the fence
1994
LLOYD FOX

Above. *Preakness gentry, decorous guests of corporate leaders and politicians, watch the horses at the finish line. Plebians, a raucous crowd on the north side of the infield, have too much fun to care.*

Rounding the bend
1996
KENNETH K. LAM

Opposite. *8-1 longshot Louis Quatorze doesn't waste any time taking the lead. The colt stayed out front from start to finish ...*

Triumphant
1996
LLOYD FOX

... providing jockey Pat Day, right, *with his fifth Preakness victory.*

Football and Baltimore. A football team bearing the Colts' name may be physically in Indianapolis, at least for now, but spiritually the franchise remains in Baltimore, and will remain so. A team called the Ravens may in time capture the hearts and minds of Marylanders, but there remains, strong and steadfast, a secure niche for the Baltimore Colts of yore. Here we see a championship team in the making, an up-and-coming 1957 team getting a briefing from coach Weeb Eubank. Many pictured here formed the nucleus of the 1958-1959 Super Bowl winners, a feat repeated in a 1971 last hurrah before baseball and the Birds came to the fore. Photo by Richard Stacks, 1957.

Dark of night
1984
LLOYD PEARSON

Above. *Amid snow flurries and hometown tears, moving trucks execute a surprise evacuation of the Colts' training site on March 28, 1984, as hated owner Robert Irsay defects to Indianapolis.*

Hero worship
1960
RICHARD STACKS

Opposite. *Ever accommodating, ever popular, ever remembered, Colts gridiron commander in chief, quarterback Johnny Unitas, signs autographs for three young admirers.*

Ravin' for the Ravens
1998

JOHN MAKELY

Above. *Cheerleaders run out onto the field before the start of the first season at the new Ravens roost just south of the Orioles nest at Camden Yards.*

Football fanfare
1998

KARL MERTON FERRON

Opposite. *The Ravens Marching Band tunes up before strutting out on the field for the first football game ever played in their new stadium.*

Got it!
1998
LLOYD FOX

Above. *A high school clash between the Bryn Mawr School and Notre Dame Prep shows that robust lacrosse is not a male monopoly in Maryland.*

Maryland's game
1995
JED KIRSCHBAUM

Right. *As the acknowledged world citadel of lacrosse, the state fields some of the best teams and fiercest rivalries anywhere. The 1995 University of Maryland squad celebrates an upset over Johns Hopkins, which is to lacrosse what Notre Dame is to football.*

Dynamic Dunbar
1996
MICHAEL LUTZKY

Above. Perennial incubator for basketball greats, Baltimore's Dunbar High School wins another state championship as its hoopsters celebrate victory over the Kennedy Cavaliers of Montgomery County.

Pickup game
1992
MARK BUGNASKI

Opposite.
Future College Park star Keith S. Booth dribbles past his two little brothers on Lafayette Courts in East Baltimore.

Over the rainbow
1994
KARL MERTON FERRON

A bat, a ball, a boy ... and as if that is not enough, 7-year-old Brian Vazzanno finds a rainbow in the sky and a diamond on the ground as Owings Mills opens its instructional league.

PLACE

By FRANK P. L. SOMERVILLE

Maryland's landmarks need not survive to exert their influence. Buildings once disdained and demolished without a thought to their worth take on vivid new life in the memories of reformers determined to save what is left.

In 1964, bureaucrats razed overnight the high-Victorian facade of Broadway Market. It had formed a gateway to Fells Point for exactly 100 years. The outcry prompted Baltimore Mayor Theodore R. McKeldin to order that henceforth no demolition of a city-owned landmark could occur without an evaluation by a new preservation commission.

Definitions of the word "landmark" have changed through the centuries almost as much as the panorama of architectural fashions it came to legitimize.

Its first recorded use was some 1,000 years ago, when it meant literally an object that marked the land, such as a stone set on a boundary. Treasured examples dating from the 1760s can be found today along the Mason-Dixon Line separating Maryland from Pennsylvania.

To some local traditionalists, such a stone is more than a landmark; it separates the geographical and cultural South from the rest of the nation.

Meanwhile, the word was developing along another track. It was used for anything conspicuous that distinguished a place and served as a guide, as for mariners on the Chesapeake Bay searching the horizon.

In the 19th century it evolved further and came to mean a turning point, or a characteristic of historical significance. The distinction of age could be part of its meaning.

There are usages that the word's first users never dreamed of. Landmark (meaning precedent-shattering) legislation is enacted, among other things, to protect landmark buildings, seen as examples of an earlier, more refined taste, a more pleasing scale, a more beautiful cityscape. "Architecture sums up the civilization it enshrines," said philosopher-critic Lewis Mumford, "and the mass of our buildings can never be better or worse than the institutions that have shaped them."

Environmental concerns equated with architectural preservation have become a moral imperative for growing numbers of Marylanders. Jane Jacobs' persuasive arguments in favor of crowded, lively, thus safer, more humane city streets coalesced with Ada Louise Huxtable's eclectic architectural preferences.

When Mumford took part in the 1961 dedication of the new Baltimore Life Insurance Building on Howard Street, the first privately financed project in the Mount Royal urban renewal area, he called on Maryland's business and professional leaders to emulate the far-sighted merchants of Venice and Amsterdam by living "in the city" and "for the city."

Make Baltimore "rich in gardens, open spaces and fine buildings," he urged. Mumford did not foresee that within a few decades the owners of the new structure would move their operations to the suburban sprawl of Owings Mills. The state would take over the property, board up its doors and windows, and slate it for demolition as "an eyesore to the community too long."

So, with few exceptions, the state's man-made landmarks, even the most honored among them and despite their number and variety, lead tenuous existences, subject always to economic pressures.

Which of them have the greatest claim on immortality? Probably some of the houses of worship that have mirrored their builders' highest aspirations through 365 years of Maryland's religious history. Arches and spires dedicated to God shaped rural villages in the 23 counties as well as the cities.

The clapboard, shuttered, hushed simplicity of Easton's Third Haven Meeting House has inspired and reassured Quakers since 1684.

In East Baltimore, the 1845 Lloyd Street Synagogue, oldest in Maryland and third-oldest in the country, is the Classic Revival cornerstone of an ambitious Jewish museum.

Of Stanford White's innovative 1887 Lovely Lane United Methodist Church, Mumford wrote in "The Brown Decades," his study of the arts from 1865 to 1895, that the imposing Italianate tower of granite on St. Paul Street "is surely one of the finest that has been erected in America."

For unequivocal scholarly praise for a Baltimore landmark, however, nothing could beat Sir Nikolaus Pevsner's. In an "American Postscript" to his major 1943 treatise on European architecture, he states flatly that the porticoed Basilica of the Assumption, the nation's first Roman Catholic cathedral, is "North America's most beautiful church."

When the entire town of Annapolis, Maryland's capital since 1694, was designated a National Historic Landmark in 1965 by the Department of the Interior, Secretary Stewart Udall declared, "Annapolis has the greatest concentration of 18th-century buildings anywhere in the United States." Affluence and self-interested vigilance as much as preservation statutes have been necessary to protect that legacy.

Wye Oak
1973
PAUL M. HUTCHINS

There wasn't even a place on the map
called Wye Mills, or a Talbot County,
over four and a half centuries ago when
the Wye Oak pushed its first tendril
above the loam of the Eastern Shore.
Who could have foreseen that one day
it would be celebrated as the most ven-
erable on this continent among that
tribe of long-lived trees, the white
oaks? Who could have guessed it would
still be pushing its many arms heaven-
ward, even into another millennium?

Bromo Seltzer Tower
1931
PHOTOGRAPHER UNKNOWN

Awareness flashed in his mind like lightning that hot June day in 1995. John Williams, retired construction worker and regular sidewalk superintendent at the site of the new Convention Center annex rising from a ditch between Conway and Pratt streets, suddenly realized he was probably older than every edifice within his view along Pratt Street and beyond, that, in fact, he had helped build some of them.

"Except for that one," he said, pointing to the Bromo Seltzer Tower, rising above Pratt and Eutaw, a graceful, poignant counterpoint to its brusque, square-shouldered neighbors.

Built in 1911, the tower has been a part of Baltimore's image from the moment it appeared on the skyline. It was once the highest structure in the city, higher even than it is today, when it supported its famous blue bottle, as shown here. The tower survived the controlled annihilation of the downtown in the 1960s. It will travel with us into the new millennium. Some regard it as Baltimore's unofficial emblem, a Renaissance tower for a renaissance city, and a giddy flourish from times far more staid than these.

The Washington Monument
1996
THOMAS GRAVES

Above. *For a gray winter city, the elegant gift of snow and holiday lights.*

Guarding the art
1996
JED KIRSCHBAUM

Opposite. *One of those who keep an eye on those eyeing the art at the Walters Gallery.*

Glory
1991
AMY DEPUTY

Opposite. *Voices rise to the vaulted roof of Bethel AME Church, a stately structure built in 1910. One of the oldest of African-American congregations, Bethel at century's end is 214 years old.*

Praise
1950
JOESEPH DIPAOLA, JR.

Above. *Altar boys Samuel Donohue and Phillip Muth look towards the towers of the Basilica of the National Shrine of the Assumption of the Blessed Virgin Mary. Construction began in 1806 and was completed in 1821.*

Storm over Federal Hill
1934
PHOTOGRAPHER UNKNOWN

Every flag has a language of its own, which it speaks to the people who brought it into being, those who chose its colors, had it stitched and sewn, who devised the arrangement of stars and stripes, or fields of red or blue, its flourishes, insignia, marks of heraldry, the other codes of nationhood. The language of the flag is an emotional one. It calls forth high sentiments; it celebrates selflessness. It becomes known, this language, almost without conscious instruction to each generation as it comes along. And as each generation passes, the flag is there. The flag evokes the same response among the most disparate people from all across the territory that is the flag's ordained purview. It discriminates not at all among those it was created to speak to; it is utterly inclusive and offers itself equally to all. No one can own the flag, yet everybody does.

Fort McHenry
1947
HANS MARX

Above: *In the winter silence the veteran cannon are still on guard. Has the British fleet returned? Is it circling in the mist, as it did before being driven off in the War of 1812? They left behind a Baltimore flush with victory and a nation with a new anthem.*

Calvert Street
1904
PHOTOGRAPHER UNKNOWN

Could you believe it? A time when there were more horses on Calvert Street than people, let alone cars.

Patapsco
State Park
1924
**H. ARMSTRONG
ROBERTS**

*An afternoon
on the Patapsco's
gentle bank at
summer's end,
full of joy in life's
bright morning.*

The library is the University of the Common Man. It is a cultural fortress, a castle keep where the true treasures of civilization are secured and made available to anyone with the desire to seize them. The library embraces everything that is human. An account of every experience ever had by men and women, be it bright or dark, tragic or thrilling, is on record somewhere in the library. It is where one goes to learn about the way things end, and the way they begin. It is a place, literally, and in the case of this 1996 photo by Jed Kirschbaum, symbolically, of reflection.

Wedding in
the Pratt
Central library
1998

ANDRE F. CHUNG

*There is no bet-
ter place for two
people, in love with
books and each
other, to bring
about their own
beginning.*

Mason-Dixon Line marker
1956
A. AUBREY BODINE

    Above. *A fading sign of a once fatal divide, in Hagerstown.*

Covered bridge
1976
CLARENCE B. GARRETT

    Opposite. *Out of the dark and into the weak light of a mountain fall day, in Utica.*

Sugarloaf Mountain
1955
RICHARD STACKS

    Overleaf. *An expanse of light, shadow and space, the earth swells above the Frederick County landscape.*

**2600 block of
Wilkins Ave.
1952**

A. AUBREY BODINE

*It is the longest row
of houses in a city
famous for its rowhouses.
It runs 1,180 feet, from
end to end, and includes
29 houses and 400 feet of
old church property. A
resident, so proud, once
said that people riding
by would stop and gaze
at this unvarying line of
dwellings. It had been "a
tourist attraction."*

The Bay Bridge
1950
HANS MARX

Cables turn, taut, and join Maryland shore to shore. The first bridge reached across the Chesapeake Bay in a gentle, 4-mile arc. It opened July 31, 1952. Twenty years later a second span followed the same curving course. It opened June 28, 1973. With these bridges, Maryland was truly joined from shore to shore. Above, a bridge worker takes a break.

Faith
1996
JED KIRSCHBAUM

Grayson Gilbert was six, his pancreatic cancer in remission, when after a visit to Johns Hopkins he asked his mother to take him to the Christ statue at the hospital. There he left a note.

EPILOGUE

By FREDERICK N. RASMUSSEN

Theodore Roosevelt had been president only two weeks in September of 1901, the moment when *The Sun* introduced the art of photography to its pages.

Before the century began, *The Sun*, like most newspapers, was composed of oceans of gray type. The visual boredom was occasionally relieved by a hand-drawn and hand-lettered map or pen-and-ink illustration.

The Sun, founded in 1837, did not publish its first map until October 17, 1846. It detailed the Battle of Monterey during the Mexican War. And it wasn't until the 1880s, that pen-and-ink illustrations of people and buildings began to be published with any regularity.

On September 30, 1901, readers of *The Sun* were no doubt astonished when they opened their papers that morning to see a photograph of Chief Judge James McSherry of the Maryland Court of Appeals.

There, in profile, and a rather stiff one at that, the judge appears wearing gold rimless glasses and a meticulously trimmed set of van-dyke whiskers. He is dressed formally in a wing collar, ascot tie and satin-lapeled Prince Albert frock coat.

This first photograph was not used to illustrate a story of earth-shaking relevancy but rather to accompany a rather mundane piece announcing the beginning of the court's fall term.

Despite being an event of monumental technological proportions, certainly as great if not equal to that of the application of telegraphy to news gathering which *The Sun* pioneered, readers had to search in vain to find any explanation of what greeted them that morning.

The Sun would never be the same again. In the days that followed, pictures began being used with greater frequency. With the use of photography came the birth of an entirely new department called "photographic."

In addition to providing pictures for *The Sun* and *The Evening Sun*, staff photographers also provided material for the sepia-toned photogravure section of the *Sunday Sun* still fondly remembered as the "brown section." The 1946 birth of the *Sun Magazine* created another venue for staff photographers.

For many years, photographers often were former copy boys who were drafted from other departments such as commercial photography.

"A. Aubrey Bodine came from commercial," said Walter McCardell, a veteran *Sun* photographer who spent his days as a young staff member accompanying Bodine on assignments. He tells this favorite story:

"In the days before flash bulbs, flash powder was used to create a burst of light. One day, Frank Miller, a staff photographer, was in the Belvedere Hotel using flash powder and managed to set the ballroom curtains on fire," said McCardell who retired in 1990 after a 44-year career.

Camera equipment in those early years included Kodak 4-by-5 view cameras which were later replaced by the classic Speed Graflex of "Front Page" fame. Today, photographers use 35-millimeter and digital cameras.

Dark rooms full of aromatic chemicals and red lights warning intruders that film was exposed are a thing of the past. Today, film is processed and then scanned into a computer. There are no longer drying prints hanging from dark room clotheslines.

There have also been other changes, too. Today, the photo department is no longer strictly a white male preserve since minorities and women have joined the staff.

Sunpaper photographers have covered not only Maryland but the whole world, recording wars, disasters and triumphs.

Robert F. Kniesche, an internationally recognized photographer, who began his career as a *Sun* photographer in the Twenties and later was chief of photography from 1946 until retiring in 1970, gained notoriety as an aerial cameraman.

For many years it was quite common for Kniesche to go flying over Maryland in a bi-plane snapping pictures all along the way. He was also known for his aerial views of Baltimore City.

Perhaps one of the greatest photo legends in Maryland was *Sun* photographer LeRoy B. Merriken, who joined the newspaper in 1924 and retired in 1980.

Merriken, who had started his career in 1914 with the old Baltimore American, was known not only for his famous picture of Babe Ruth at the old Oriole Park but also for covering 70 opening days.

The one unchanging constant is not the camera, the film or the computer. It is the eye of the photographer gazing through the lens with finger poised on the shutter ready to catch and preserve fleeting moments of human drama.

First photo
1901

PHOTOGRAPHER UNKNOWN

On September 30, 1901, The Sun moved into the era of news photography by publishing its first picture — a portrait of a prominent judge.

ACKNOWLEDGEMENTS

The staff of "The Century in The Sun" gratefully appreciates the help of many people without whose assistance, patience and knowledge this book would not have been possible.

A special thanks is extended to the staffs of *The Baltimore Sun* photography and library departments.

We are especially indebted to Jim Preston, David M. Lewis and Robert K. Hamilton of the *The Baltimore Sun* photography department for sharing their expertise.

Thanks are also in order for the following people: The family of A. Aubrey Bodine, John Beck and Tom Beck of University of Maryland Baltimore County Photographic Collections, Tiffany H. House, Bert Fox, Victor Panichkul and Peter Yuill.

We offered our profound appreciation to the former *Baltimore Sun* photographers who allowed us to visit their homes and pore through historic prints: Mark Bugnaski, Joseph DiPaola Jr., Clarence M. Garrett, Dave Harp, Paul M. Hutchins, Garo Lachinian, Michael Lutzky, Ellis Malashuk, Lloyd Pearson, and Irving J. Phillips, Jr.

Special thanks to James H. Bready for his knowledge of sports history in Baltimore and to Gilbert Sandler for checking historical accuracy.

Thanks to Frances Rudner for her copy-editing experitise.

Any errors or omissions are the responsibility of its editors, not of those who so generously assisted the book staff.

The construction of this book required long hours. The editors are grateful for the support and patience of their families, especially Darlene Hutchinson, Lea Jones and William Jones, throughout the process.